How Real Estate Developers Think

A practical guide with the secrets of the greatest masters and mistakes to avoid to not fail in your business

Neal Hooper

TABLE OF CONTENTS

Masters Mind State

Real Transformation Through Renovation

You finally managed to get your hands on that sweet ownership title - congratulations are in order! But before you celebrate your success, keep in mind that the

battle has only just begun. Oh, humble flipper - there's a whole lot left to do if you want to turn that title into profit, and it starts with your renovation. Renovating an old home restores value because it makes the property livable and aesthetically appealing. After all - no one could ever see themselves living in a run-down shack! Buyers gravitate towards fresh coats of paint and clean new tiles, so it's essential to make those changes if you want to reel in buyers without having to push such a hard sell. Just like the home selection process, there are a few guidelines you should keep in mind when planning out a renovation. These key points should help direct you towards making the right choices, so you get the best returns out of your effort without having to spend more than you're willing to or capable of.

The Foundations of A Cost-Effective Renovation

Understanding what is needed and what is considered a luxury will help set boundaries and keep your budget out of the red. As a general rule, you'll want to do the least without sacrificing build quality and aesthetics. It will help keep your project within reasonable cost and time limits without affecting your prospective buyers' appeal.

Know When To DIY

We're not all home improvement experts, so you will need to hire a contractor somewhere down the line, but do you? Perhaps during your own homeownership experience, you've had to oversee a few home improvements projects on your own.

These likely ranged from simple repainting jobs to woodworking and everything in between. Whatever the case, it was cheaper to get it done by yourself and a few subcontractors instead of hiring a general contractor to do the job for you.

Unfortunately, the decision to push through as a DIY contractor might change if the house you're dealing with will be sold for a profit. But then again, get-ting it done DIY means you can cut back on the cost and increase your net profit. So, what do you do?

There are a few things you can ask yourself if you want to find out whether you're ready to take on the job of a DIY contractor. Understanding where you stand in terms of these factors will give you a realistic idea regarding your readiness and capability to oversee the operations yourself.

Do you have the time and availability to be present on-site throughout the renovation process?

Are you comfortable working with your hands and getting things done using power tools, construction materials, etc.?

Are the repairs and renovations required within your set of skills?

Do you have contacts with subcontractors to do more tedious, technical jobs for you?

Do you possess some knowledge of home improvement and renovation?

Are you confident in your capability to generate outcomes comparable to a professional contractor given the tasks you intend to do yourself?

If you answered no to any of these questions, you might be better off seeking a pro. Look - we're not underestimating your capabilities, and, indeed, everyone can learn to get home improvements done DIY-style. But taking a gamble with investment could mean more expenses down the line.

If you end up ruining any part of the repairs, you might have to call in a pro anyway and end up making extra payments for more renovations than you initially required.

Even if you manage to get the repairs done all by yourself, there's quality. Does it look like something a potential buyer would be happy to see and pay for? Or will it likely deter prospective purchasers? If it doesn't improve your property's saleability, you'd have to get a contractor anyway to clean things up for you.

Don't let the allure of saving 10% - 30% on renovation costs get the best of you - you should know what's best for your property! If you feel that you're biting off more than you can chew, you probably are.

Start With Bare Minimum

Remember - you're not aiming to create the upcoming Better Homes and Gardens featured property. So, don't go overboard with the changes you want to make.

Generally, suppose you followed the right steps in the home selection process. In that case, the layout of your home should be suitable enough to work off without changing anything about the blueprint - which leads us to a guiding mantra in the process of fixing a flip.

Focus on the cosmetic.

Nicked paint, yellowish grout, broken tiles, leaky ceilings, old bathroom fixtures, creaky cabinet and cupboard doors, and other features that might make the home look unappealing should be the focus of your efforts. These don't make any changes to the property's overall footprint and are generally cheaper to get done.

If you got your home from an auction and you weren't able to give it a closer inspection before sealing the deal, you might find a few structural damages when you finally get to walk inside.

Issues concerning windows, weight-bearing beams, rotten walls, damaged roofing, and other home features with something to do with the house's framework can be setbacks in terms of both time and cost. It's also worth mentioning that these repairs typically- quire different permits before they can be started. So that adds to the expense on top of lengthening your timeline.

Again, it's worth reiterating that the house you choose will be pivotal to your project's profitability. Make the wrong choice at the start, and you might find yourself scrambling to figure out whether you can make a profit at all.

The 4 Kinds of Home Renovations

There are four different kinds of renovations that you can execute on your property, and each of these increases the value and salability of your investment. Understanding which ones you need will help you come up with a plan that maximizes your property's AFV without having to spend too much of your budget.

The Basics

Necessary renovations are changes and repairs that address features that buyers expect should be in good order. Ceilings that don't drip and leak in the rain, functional gutters and downspouts, a working furnace, and other fundamental aspects should be in good working condition if you want to attract buyers. You don't necessarily have to renovate them all to the highest standards - simple maintenance tasks and a few minor changes to get everything working can be more than enough. Now the question - does basic renovation add value to your property? Not exactly. Buyers expect that houses for sale should have all of these basics to be considered viable options. Essentially, making sure that all of your investment's necessary features are operational simply brings your home up to standards. So, should you get them done? Absolutely. If your home doesn't have all of these basics adequately addressed, then you might not be able to reel in any buyers in the first place.

Curb Appeal

These renovations improve the aesthetic appeal of your property. Again, they don't necessarily add value, but they will help make your house sell faster. Investing in these changes can make your property look handsome and inviting from the moment buyers take a glance, making it easier for them to visualize their life there and hopefully develop an attachment that drives profitable action. Renovations that improve curb appeal include a well-manicured lawn, fresh coats of exterior and interior paint, clean carpets, and other cosmetic changes that make the place look neat and appealing. Keep in mind, though, that some curb appeal changes might only really appeal to you. So instead of trying to flex your interior design muscle, try to keep it simple. Neutral paint colors, a tasteful backsplash, and straightforward, clean bathroom tiles with white grout can be better than trying to impress buyers with your taste in unconventional bohemian inspired design.

Value-Adding

Now we move on to the aspect of renovation that improves the ARV of your investment. These changes focus on the house features that make it easier or more convenient to live in. For instance, houses with updated HVAC systems that are eco- friendly and energy-efficient are likely to save their homeowner the added expense of clunky, outdated systems. The same goes for ranges and range hoods that are more efficient at saving electricity and eliminating foul odors from the interior space. Value-adding renovations can be expensive at the get-go, so you might think they're not necessary as a beginner.

But because these changes can recoup up to 80% of their value once resale comes around, they can be incredibly beneficial for your endeavor.

Remember to stay within limits, though. Even if these changes add value, you don't want to be too different from the other houses in your vicinity. If you have state-of-the-art everything and the houses around scream plain vanilla, your home might stick out in the wrong way.

Preferential

This house would look so much better with a game room in place of that third bedroom!

Before you okay the renovation, ask yourself if this something you prefer, or is it a change that would get the thumbs up from anyone?

One major pitfall that many beginners succumb to when flipping their first house is treating it like home. The last thing you'd want is to make the mistake of developing an attachment to your investment, which might push you to make decisions that appeal more to your sense of "practicality" and "improvement" instead of the market's concept of the ideal. Again, the best way to stay grounded when planning out those changes is by checking out the competition.

If most of the houses for sale in the area have three bedrooms and no game rooms, you'd be better off the following suit.

Other changes that fit into this category include hot tubs, wine cellars, swimming pools, and ponds. Not everyone wants them, and some might be a maintenance nightmare, making them a downside for practical buyers who want a home that's not hard to live in or keep in good condition.

Four Rules For A Successful Fix-And- Flip

Do This For A Fun Flip.

House flips are more likely to fail (be unprofitable) than succeed, especially for beginners. Renovations always take longer to complete and cost more than expected,

leaving investors in the hole if they haven't anticipated setbacks. Besides, it's much harder to fix-and-flip a house than it looks on TV, and many novice flippers are shocked when they find out the extent of necessary work and the possibility that they could lose money on the deal.

To give yourself the best possible chance of success, you'll have to take a hard look at your goals, abilities, and availability. Learn everything you can before you snap up what seems like an ideal property and get stuck with a loser.

Know Your Commitment Level

Before you dive into the fix-and-flip life, sit down and think about how much you're willing and able to commit to this undertaking.

If you're going all-in on a DIY rehab, make sure you have the skills and experience you need to be successful. Renovating a house involves grueling physical work and dedication to the project.

So honestly answer these questions before you decide to take this path:

- Are you able to do contractor-quality work?

- Do you know which permits you need?

- Are you aware of all local building codes?

- Do you have subcontractors to handle repairs you aren't qualified to make?

- Do you have enough cash saved to cover higher-than- expected costs?

Even if you're not planning to do all the work yourself, fixing and flipping a house requires a considerable time commitment, and the more involved you are in the process, the more significant that commitment will need to be. While it is possible to work a full-time job and rehab properties, it's not ideal. Properties undergoing renovations need daily check-ins, preferably when the contractor is on-site. If you can only get to the property after work and after the contractor (or foreman) has left for the day, you're more likely to run into problems and delays—and that will lead to shrinking profits.

Consider A Flip Mentor

Seek out a successful flipper and ask if she or he'd be open to mentoring you. You'll gain valuable knowledge and experience that would otherwise take years (and lots of failures) to learn. To increase your chance of "yes," consider offering the flipper a small portion of the profits on your first successful flip.

Gather Pros To Cover The Gaps

Chances are, you're not a real estate agent and a CPA and a real estate lawyer and a contractor. For any area in which you're not an expert, hire a professional. There are many intricacies involved in a successful house-flipping investment, and if you

don't know what you're doing, your dreams of large profits can turn into mountains of debt.

If you are planning on doing as much of the fix-up work as possible on your own, don't cut costs when it comes to make- or-break parts of the project. Even seasoned contractors call on licensed professionals to fill in experience gaps. Ensure you know what kind of help you'll need and take steps to secure it before you get started.

Have A Cash Stash

Financing your flip with cash (or mostly cash) increases your profit potential. Not only will you save thousands of dollars in loan fees and interest, but you'll also be in a better position if the house takes longer than expected to fix or flip (which almost always happens, especially in the beginning).

Remember, to be profitable, and the sales price has to exceed the total purchase price, carrying costs (insurance, loan interest, utilities, etc.), and renovation expenses. Cutting down borrowing costs—interest, loan application and settlement fees, mortgage insurance—leaves more money to invest in renovations. Plus, having a sizable down payment for the property can get you better terms for any money you need to borrow.

Make The Right Renovations

Property
Comparisons

	47 Suffolk Street Medford, MA 02155	2 Ronaele Rd Medford, MA 02155
MLS #	70525053	71381143
Status	Sold	Sold
List Price	$499,900	$399,999
Sale Price	$499,900	$395,000
List Date	2/12/2007	5/10/2012
Off Market Date	3/14/2007	9/10/2012
Sale Date	3/30/2007	10/18/2012
Days on Market	30	123
Style	Colonial, Gambrel /Dutch	Multi-Level
Bedrooms	3	3
Full Baths	1	1
Half Baths	0	1
Total Rooms	8	8
Square Feet	1856	1759
Acres	0.17	0.16
Lot Size (sq.ft.)	7544	6840
Year Built	1926	1960
Fireplaces	1	1
Garage Spaces	1	1
Garage Desc	Detached, Garage Door Opener	Attached, Under
Basement Desc	Full, Interior Access, Concret...	Full, Finished, Walk Out, Inte...
Int. Features	Cable Available, Walk-up Attic	Security System, Cable Available
Ext. Features	Deck, Patio, Gutters, Sprinkle...	Porch - Enclosed, Patio, Gutte...
Sewer & Water	City/Town Water	
Waterfront		
Beach Desc	Lake/Pond	
Assessed Value	$474,800	$351,900
Taxes	$4,220.97	$4,233
Tax Year	2007	2012

It's tempting to create a dream house with hardwood floors and top-of-the-line appliances, but that kind of thinking will put you on the fast track to flip failure. When it comes to renovations, you want to make only those that will add value— not just look good. Small tweaks can make a significant, cost- effective impact: for example, painting and putting new hardware on cabinets can add as much value as installing new cabinets but at a fraction of the cost.

Remember, the less you spend on renovations, the bigger your investment returns will be. Before you dive in, learn how much typical projects cost. Know what you'll pay to re-carpet a house, update old wiring, and spruce up the landscaping.

While every flip project is different, some upgrades that almost always add value include:

- Updating kitchen appliances

- Upgrading the washer and dryer

- Repainting inside and outside

- Adding closet space

- Building a deck

- Adding a bathtub (if there isn't one)

Depending on the area, bringing in some green energy features can increase the home value—but make sure there's a positive "going green" vibe in the neighborhood before you take on the extra expense.

Repairs Are Not Renovations

While you may decide to go lower budget on renovations, don't skimp on necessary repairs. Anything that involves building codes or safety should be done professionally, and anything that's broken should be fixed.

First Impressions Matter

The first thing someone sees when they're viewing your property is the outside ("curb appeal"). A neat yard and a fresh coat of paint make a good first impression and convince the buyer to walk inside.

Simple touches can help add to the curb appeal, and most of these can be done (as needed) without shelling out a lot of cash:

- Make sure the trim work is freshly painted

- Paint the front door or add new hardware

- Install outdoor lighting

- Plant seasonal flowers

- Repair cracks in the driveway and walkways

- Put in a new mailbox

These minor fix-ups won't bust your budget, but they will help draw buyers to the house.

Price The House Properly

It can be tempting to price your flip house based on how much money you want to make, but if you don't want the house to sit there unsold, you'll need to come up with a realistic, competitive price.

To avoid excessive lag times and the drag of having to keep lowering your price (which can make potential buyers think there's something wrong with the property and bypass it altogether), set your price in keeping with the appropriate comps in the neighborhood. You can also order an appraisal to get an objective view of the property value.

Be aware that other things will come into play when you're ready to sell. For example, homes sell better in spring than winter. A glut of homes for sale in the same area makes it harder to get your asking price; a lack of for-sale homes will make it easier. Bottom line: be realistic about the possible sales price range before you buy your investment property.

Strategic Pricing

When people are looking for houses, they usually search in a price range. Those ranges are often measured in ten- (sometimes five-) thousand-dollar increments (such as

$220,000 to $230,000), so a home price at the top of a range gets as much play as a lower price. If you decide to lower your price, move it down enough to change its range (for example, reduce it to $219,000 rather than $220,000); that way, your audience will be expanded to include people searching in the new range.

Pay Attention to Comps

Before you set a price, look at what other neighborhood homes are selling for, especially those with similar characteristics to your investment property. The best way to do that is by viewing "comps," data from a comparative market analysis (CMA), readily available to real estate agents. To make your accurate comp list, include these filters in your search (on any real estate sales website):

- Within a half-mile radius from your property

- Current listings (no older than three months)

- Similar square footage (within 10 %)

- Similar age

You can also go online and get a "Zestimate" based on Zillow's home market value estimator.

(While you're there, make sure that all the information listed is correct since millions of people use Zillow as a starting point for home buying.)

Consider Incentives

In an area with similar homes for sale, offering an incentive can set your property apart from the pack. Possible incentives include offering six months of prepaid homeowners' association dues, paying buyer closing costs, or paying for the home inspection.

Protect Your Investment

It's best not to purchase property in your name for your protection but use a holding company instead. That serves the dual purpose of shielding your assets from any liabilities arising

from the business property (like a contractor being hurt) and protecting your investment from being lost to a personal judgment (like a tax lien).

At the same time, you can reap other benefits by creating a holding company for your investment properties, such as:

• Extra tax advantages

- Simplified accounting

- Streamlined transfers to heirs

The key to cementing that protection is to keep personal and business finances completely separate.

For example, that means never using a personal credit card to buy renovation supplies at Home Depot.

If your flipping business needs cash, make a formal contribution to the company rather than paying the contractor with your check.

Also, treat your business like a business: run it professionally and following all federal, state, and local laws. Keep your bookkeeping up to date. And while you can form these companies DIY, it's better (especially if you're working with partners) to have an experienced real estate lawyer set it up for you.

Make Sure to Be Fully Insured

A lot can go wrong during renovations, and bulletproof insurance coverage will be your first defense line if disaster strikes.

Insurance for fix-and-flip properties can be expensive, making many flipping newbies shy away from complete coverage.

The goal is to balance the cost of premiums with the benefits you're getting buy the right kinds and the right amount of coverage.

It can be tricky because some insurance companies won't want to cover vacant properties, and coverage you do find can be much more expensive than regular homeowners' insurance.

In addition to vacant (or unoccupied) property coverage, house flippers should consider purchasing:

- Fire and hazard coverage

- Sewer/septic backup coverage

- Vandalism and theft insurance

- Errors and omissions (E/O) coverage (professional liability insurance)

- Workers compensation insurance (if there are employees like a building super or maintenance workers on-site)

- Flood insurance (depending on where your property is situated—like at the bottom of a hill or in a flood plain)

- Umbrella insurance (to cover anything not covered by other policies)

Some companies may combine these policies in one significant policy, but make sure your coverage is as comprehensive as possible.

You can look online to check out real estate investment insurance offerings on the National Real Estate Insurance

Group. If you aren't sure which insurance coverage your investment property needs, work with a professional who has flipping experience. Visit the National Association of Insurance Commissioners at www.naic.org to find a reputable agent.

Neal Hooper

Build Your Pipeline

I told you it is all about activity and not so much about the outcome. However, if you do the work, you will invariably get an outcome without even trying: you will have a

pipeline of deals and investors, and have your team on the ground ready to go.

The "Pipeline Step" is all about continuing to make offers and raising money to build your pipeline. And the bigger your pipeline, the faster you'll do your first deal.

In addition to making offers, you'll also have to deal with mental challenges to survive.

Keys to Surviving Real Estate Investing in Flipping Houses

After a few months, the excitement begins to wane, and the entrepreneur becomes frustrated by the apparent lack of progress. As a result, many give up their quest for financial freedom for two primary reasons:

#1: Lack of support and community

#2: Delays, setbacks, and challenges

I've found that these feelings of despair affect every entrepreneur at one time or another—sometimes more than once. The key is how you respond to them. Let's drill down on each of these so that you're in the best position to handle and overcome them.

Reason #1: Lack of Support and Community

Being a real estate entrepreneur seeking your first flipped house deal is a lonely sport. Chances are you don't have a single friend or family member who has done what you want to do. Many of your friends and family members think you're crazy and are doing nothing to encourage you on your journey.

Then there's the issue of who to turn to when you have a question.

Even the best course or seminar won't address every possible situation you might encounter, because every deal is different. Who can you turn to when you have a question? Are you buying, right? Are you too eager to do a deal? What should you do about the mold issue you uncovered during due diligence? Many of these questions can paralyze you if you don't have someone to turn to for support. The key to succeeding in this step is to get some help and join a community of like-minded entrepreneurs.

But not to worry! Here are three tips to help you overcome this challenge.

Tip #1: Find an accountability partner. It's a proven fact that only ten will take action for every one hundred people who attend a seminar. If you're one of the 90% of people who don't naturally stick with something after they start it, you will need an accountability partner, someone who will encourage you and keep you accountable. This person could be a spouse, friend, or someone you pay (like a coach or mentor).

It doesn't matter which one you seek out, but you must align yourself with a person like that. Otherwise, your efforts will peter out sooner. So make sure you have an accountability partner.

Tip #2: Surround yourself with like-minded people.

It is the same flipping house start-up business. Make sure you encircle yourself with like-minded entrepreneurs working toward identical goals and can help you.

On fine days, you enjoy sharing your triumphs. But who can truly comprehend and value what you've achieved? And on bad days, you must have somebody to advise you that it will be alright, that it's all valuable, keep pushing. Who comprehends what we've been going through? Right, very few individuals, specifically our family and friends.

That's why you must pursue out like-minded entrepreneurs.

Again, it doesn't count as much what sort of community you keep, but it does matter that you're a portion of one. It could be a mastermind group. Perhaps you make one from the individuals you encounter at the boot camp or possibly spend to enter one. In-person is most acceptable, but a virtual community is an extraordinary (and often more sensible) option. It will provide the longevity of your efforts and the eventual success of your business.

Tip #3: Find a mentor. Top athletes have coaches. Top actors have coaches. Even the most successful business people have coaches.

I recommend that you build an "advisory board" of more experienced investors—they are invaluable. However, I've found that you're not going to get the kind of support you need from "volunteer" mentors, especially in the beginning.

That's why I think it's best to hire a coach who can help you do your first deal. Not every successful real estate entrepreneur has a paid coach, but they have all had a mentor or advisor.

One of the two main reasons people quit their pursuit of a flipping house deal is that they did not address support. The solution is to find an accountability partner, start or join a like- minded community, and find an experienced mentor or coach. If you follow these tips, your chances for success skyrocket.

Reason #2: Delays, Setbacks, and Challenges

Right around three months after people decide to get started with flipping houses investing, the initial adrenaline wears off, and they become frustrated that they haven't done a deal or raised any money yet. And, frankly, it's more work than they thought it would be. They might say to themselves, "I don't think this multifamily thing works. Or maybe it works for others, but not for me."

Here are some tips for dealing with these days of doubt and discouragement.

Tip #1: Revisit yours why. Now it's time to revisit your vision map and evaluate why you decided to embark on this crazy journey in the first place. Was it to quit your job? To escape the constant pressure of having to provide for your family? Why was that important? So that you could regain control of your time to do whatever you wanted, whenever you wanted, and with whom you wanted? And why was that important? Was it perhaps to spend more time with your growing children? To improve your relationship with your spouse? To travel more?

Whatever it was for you, go back to when you decided to get started with multifamily investing. What pain were you running from? What better things did you want for yourself and your family?

If this tip doesn't keep you going, then redo your vision map. But this time, really do it. Spend time on it. Meditate over it. Involve your spouse and family.

One of my favorite quotes is from Tony Robbins: "It is in your moments of decision that your destiny is shaped."

I find that whenever a person indeed decides something, the only possible outcome is action.

Whenever I see a person not taking action and probing further, I find that the person has not settled.

They may say they want something, but they're lying to themselves and others.

It is why you must decide, right now, if you want to change your life or you want to have the same experience you have right now this time following year. But you have to decide.

Tip #2: Put things in perspective. What you're doing with is hard. It's worthwhile, but it's tough. It's not like you can get the results you want (replacing your income) in thirty days or less.

No, you have to stick with it—every week for three to five years until you can quit your job and do what you want.

While this is a long time, look at it from this perspective: your retirement plan is only three to five years. Most people have a forty-plus year retirement plan, but yours is only three to five years.

Isn't that much better? So if you're considering giving up after three months of doing this flipping houses thing, think about the timeline you're on. You know that you're on a three- to-five-year retirement plan, so clearly, three months isn't going to cut it.

But you also know that your retirement timeline is infinitely better and faster than 99% of other people out there, so it's worth it.

Okay, enough complaining. Get back to working on the plan!

Tip #3: Recognize and celebrate your (small) successes. I find in working with students that they often don't see the progress they're making.

They're so focused on doing their first deal (as they should be!) that they become discouraged when it doesn't happen in the first few months. In reality, they've made tremendous progress, and it's important to recognize this by celebrating the small successes.

Stick with It!

The key to surviving is, first and foremost, awareness. Anticipate the feelings of doubt and discouragement as you experience setbacks, challenges, and delays. An accountability partner or mentor is critical because they will guide you through these days of doubt and discouragement. They will put these feelings into perspective, remind you of your goals, highlight the progress you've already made, and encourage you to keep going.

The good news is that if you can get over this three-month hump, you're good to go. Just be aware of it, surround yourself with good support, and keep on moving forward.

Mistakes To Avoid When Starting Your Own House Flipping Business

Investing in real estate can seem like an easy way to make money; this book should have shown you that this is not the case. There is money to be made, but it takes hard

work, dedication, and patience to be successful. When first looking to invest in the property market, it is widespread to make the following mistakes:

Planning

The importance of planning cannot be overemphasized. Before any purchase is made, you must know your goals and how you intend to achieve them. One of the biggest mistakes any real estate investor can make is to attempt to make up the solution as they go along; this approach is designated to fail as they will not have the information available to make informed decisions. Instead of working out a budget, the right property type, and the location, it can be tempting to purchase a property because it looks good. Of course, this is likely to mean you will overspend and struggle to break even, never mind create a profit.

Planning is essential; you then pick the property based on the parameters you have set; the actual property is almost irrelevant! Treat property investment as what it is; a business.

Believing The Hype

Shows are abundant regarding flipping property or property development. These shows make it look effortless to transform a property and sell for a decent profit; they do not show all the scenes' hard work. The same is true for much of the literature that you find scattered around the internet. In effect, these programs make real estate investment look like a get rich quick scheme. It is not!

To be successful, you must be patient, organized, and willing to take risks; even a calculated risk in property investment can result in huge losses and even destroy all the hard work you have put in.

Doing It All Alone

It can be very tempting to choose a property, renovate it, and either find tenants or put it on the market. However, you will be missing a considerable amount of possibilities and placing your profit in jeopardy. To successfully buy and sell a property, you need an attorney, a real estate agent, and, almost certainly, a financial backer. If you intend to build a business in real estate, you will be doing these many times. The insight and assistance that these professionals can give you will make a massive difference to your business's success or failure.

On top of this, you will need builders, plumbers, and electricians to complete the renovations and annual maintenance. Building a relationship with these tradesmen will ensure you have support on hand when you need it— having the work completed by professionals will also avoid any issues with substandard work when you come to sell or lease the property.

Research

Investment properties often come up at short notice, and an investor will need to act quickly to ensure they secure the property. Unfortunately, this will provide little or no time to research the property, location, and repairs. It can be a recipe for disaster as the property could drain all your available resources; even then, you may struggle to sell it.

To ensure you are always prepared for a deal that may happen, you should continuously research the property market. It will entail monitoring current market movements, up and coming neighborhoods, and average prices for the neighborhoods within your desired vicinity. You should also make sure you know any changes in regulations that may affect the way you purchase property or the property types you are buying.

Volume

When you first start in real estate investment, it is easier to purchase a property and deal with it entirely before moving onto the subsequent. However, this is not going to turn your portfolio into a viable business. To succeed at property investment, you need to keep several deals in the pipeline at all times; this does not mean you have to complete on all of them at the same time. It does mean that you will not miss out on a once in a lifetime opportunity, and any deals that are not as good as they first appear will be seen for what they are and terminated.

Multiple Options

The property market can be extremely volatile; even seasoned professionals who have done all the necessary research can find themselves with a perfect flipping property and are now too expensive. For this reason, it is essential to have multiple options. When you plan your budget for the property, be sure to consider what you would do if you could not sell it. Renting may be an option or selling on owner finance.

The critical part of this is to be prepared and have multiple options at your disposal; then, no matter how a situation may change, you know you have a way out.

Bad Finance

By now, you will have realized that there are lots of different ways in which you can finance your subsequent property purchase. However, think carefully before signing up for any deal; in your eagerness to secure the funds, you may engage in bad finance. It does not mean there is anything wrong with the funds you receive; it merely means that the finance terms are not as attractive as those you could have chosen.

Of course, there are other reasons why you may have chosen a specific finance deal, and these reasons might outweigh the additional cost of a deal. Again, adequate research will ensure you get a good deal and do not waste part of your profit in interest charges and other ancillary costs.

Taxes

As a real estate investor, you are running a business, and you will need to record your income and expenditure, plus any other relevant charges. These figures can then be used to calculate the tax due on your earnings. It is essential to keep accurate records and be aware of each of your properties; this way, you will not be sent a tax demand that you cannot afford.

Every state has its own rules regarding taxes and real estate investors; it is vital to check your local laws and regulations to ensure you conform. It is also advisable to be aware of the

capital gains tax and how much it could cost you if you decide to sell one of your properties.

Many people find it beneficial to use the services of an accountant or financial advisor.

Self-Managing

Just like trying to do everything yourself, managing your property or properties yourself will leave you likely to fail as a real estate investor. It is because you do not have the time to look after all your tenants' demands and build your own business while staying abreast of the latest market developments.

A property manager will check potential tenants and deal with your tenants' day-to-day issues without needing to disturb you, leaving you free to focus on the bigger picture and what you need to do after that.

Deferring Maintenance

It will be incredibly tempting to save costs by not replacing a worn-out boiler until it has broken completely or until you have the funds available. However, this type of approach will cost you more in the long run. Tenants whose needs are not met will vote with their feet and leave at the end of the agreement.

It is also likely that if you do not pay out and repair something while you can, you are likely to have something else go wrong and end up needing to replace an item rather than repairing it; this will increase the drain on your finances.

Staying on top of the maintenance will help keep your tenants happy and prolong the amount of time they are likely to remain in your property.

Buying the Wrong Property

Sometimes this is an inevitable outcome and a part of the learning curve. If you have bought the wrong property for your portfolio or have limited income and tenants' potential, then the best thing you can do is offload the property as quickly as possible. It is preferable to do this for a profit but not for the same price you paid for it. It will minimize any financial impact.

A lack of research or following your heart instead of your head is the most obvious reason for buying the wrong property, but sometimes, it can actually tick all the right boxes and still be wrong. It is an experience that most real estate investors have and need to learn from and move on.

Education

Because anyone can buy and sell a house, it is often believed that it is unnecessary to have an education or be a successful real estate investor. However, as already said, this must be treated like the business it is. If you have studied business at school or college, you will be able to apply this working knowledge to the real estate industry; it will help you know how to run a business.

Educating yourself in business management will allow you to develop strategies that others have not thought of; it will ensure you look at your real estate investments as their business and provide you with a good knowledge of general business concepts.

If you did not do well at school, then there are plenty of adult course which can be completed, and education will prevent you from making many, costly mistakes.

Expectations

Real estate investment is not a get rich quick scheme, and it is not an easy option. You need to be always on the ball regarding market developments and potential properties. There will be pressures and demands from your properties and your tenants; in fact, there is probably always be something that needs your attention.

None of these challenges are insurmountable, but you must be prepared for them and prepared to work hard to make the most of your resources.

Give Up on a Bad Deal

At times you will purchase a bad deal; this can happen even if you conduct all the research and analysis possible. The important thing regarding a property which is not suitable for your portfolio is to have the courage to admit it was a wrong purchase and get it back on the market. It can sometimes be demanding as you may wish to continue to prove others wrong, or even because you are trying something different and are convinced it will work out.

Whatever the reason, it is essential to remember that your real estate investment is a business and assess each property regularly, not just when you purchase them. The global and local economy can affect your property, and what has initially been a good investment may no longer be.

The Cash Reserve

One of the biggest mistakes newcomers to the real estate industry makes to not have a cash reserve. It is essential to meet your financial obligations if your property is vacant or to make repairs in an emergency. A cash reserve also gives you the upper hand; you do not need to give in to the demands of a tenant to ensure they stay in your property; you can afford to take your time picking the right tenant and, if you decide to sell, you can hold out until you get the right offer.

What is the 70% Rule?

What is the 70% Rule?

The 70% rule says that an investor should aim to pay no more than 70% of a property's after repair value, or ARV.

it's important to use a realistic estimate of the property's value after repairs are completed and factor in an estimate of what the repairs will cost.

Purchase Right Using the 70% Rule

Some would state that when flipping houses, the sale is the most pivotal individual loan. To ensure that we do this properly with the smallest risk possible, we use ARV to decide the amount to pay for a property.

The initial phase in purchasing right is deciding your repair or recovery cost. You can do this by getting an estimate from the contractual worker you plan on employing.

When you realize your home flip repair costs, then you can begin doing your ARV investigation to figure out what you should purchase for the house.

There are various ways to do this, yet the ideal path is to utilize what we call "The 70% Rule". I've utilized the 70% guideline on many occasions. It is once in a while saved me by either dodging an awful buy or making considerable resources.

The 70% Rule in Real Life

Suppose you have decided with your specialist that the ARV of a specific house you are thinking about purchasing is

$200,000. There are a few comps in the zone, and demonstrate that $200,000 is a reasonable cost, and these ongoing deals information gives you the certainty that you can get a similar cost for your property.

So here are the means by which the 70% standard works:

1. **Decide Your 70% Rule Amount**

Take the $200,000 and double it by 70% ARV = $200,000
70% Rule: $200,000 x 0.70 = $140,000

2. **Decide Your Buy Price**

Subtract your repair costs from that $140,000.

If the repairs are $40,000, then, by utilizing the 70% principle, you realize that the maximum amount of money you need to pay for this house is $100,000.

Repair costs = $40,000 70% Rule = $140,000

$140,000 - $40,000 = $100,000

Maximum Purchase Cost = $100,000

By utilizing the 70% principle, you have now established that the maximum you need to pay for this house is $100,000.

3.   Decide Your Offer Price

$100,000 isn't your offer cost.

You will need to offer the vendor a rate beneath your 70% standard purchase cost.

Usually, we propose 20% or even 30% lower than what we intend to pay.

So right now, our initial offer is at $70,000

You'll no doubt go back and forth with the vendor, wheeling and dealing over cost and other concessions. In any case, by offering a purchase cost of 20% to 30% beneath your budget, it ensures you'll have the option to make a profit while flipping this house.

When we spread selling your home flip, you'll see why in the following segment. You may even find that the owner may acknowledge your first offer, which happens now and again, particularly if the house is troubled or the owner is looking for a quick sell.

Why the 70% Rule Works

Consider the 30% hole in the 70% principle as a security net or a pad to limit unfruitful deals and ensure you profit on the deal.

Remember that end and holding costs, along with unforeseen descending business sector weight, may leave you with less profit—however, the 70% standard protects you against potential profit misfortune.

Taxes

If you set your investment property up like a business, in the first place, it will keep you on track as you expand on your arrangement of properties. You have income and expenses that must be represented and followed, for your very own profit and state and government taxes.

You have to ascertain your income, less your expenses, to decide if you have a profit and how much in taxes might be expected. (If you have misfortune, you ought to have the option to apply it against your income.) Remember that owning speculation property gives openings and incredible tax benefits.

One of the focal points is your capacity to deduct every operating cost and deterioration from your income while estimating your speculation increases in value. Tax laws are substantially more muddled for a venture property than for an individual home.

The taxation laws are unique and change regularly, making it hard to keep up. Consequently, a significant piece of owning property is having an incredible money related organizer and a guaranteed open bookkeeper (CPA), both of whom have a lot of knowledge in real estate. You need to have a general comprehension of the taxes and what is expected, just as knowledge of various types of protection accessible to cover your most dire outcome imaginable. Also, you should be sure you're consenting to your nearby government organizations. A few urban areas or regions require uncommon licenses and yearly assessments by the city overseer or local fire-fighters for well-being and security infringement. There are commonly two types of income In the tax world: ordinary income and capital gains.

Ordinary income incorporates your wages, pay rates, rewards, commissions, profits, rental income, and intrigue income. It is taxed at different rates, contingent upon your tax part. Then again, you need to deal with the other kind of tax, capital gains, gently, because this is the tax for income created when assets, for example, real estate and stock, have been sold for a profit. Equations are set for everything in regard to ordinary income and capital gains income. You should be sure you have outstanding records and keep your administrative work sorted out, so you are prepared to meet with your bookkeeper. New tax laws and deterioration plans change frequently, and there is no chance to get for you to stay aware of everything — nor are you expected to. Discover a time to plan an arrangement for a monetary and tax survey. Plan and be readied. Get a tax methodology set up to help you choose when to improve your property and sell your venture.

Types of Taxes

There is a wide range of kinds of taxes. There are state and government taxes, neighborhood taxes, in certain spots, city or region taxes, property taxes, and those dazzling business taxes. Counsel with your accountant for subtleties, and make sure to check with your city, region, and state to be sure you are consenting to all prerequisites.

State Tax

A few states don't have a state tax, which means you're not required to do a state tax return. Explore from the state government where your property is arranged to get some answers concerning its taxes. Your accountant may have a proposal of whom to contact to acquire the most recent information or have an office in that state. Most states have an income tax and an exchange tax, accounting for considerable state land taxes. When you do your tax return and are in a state with this kind of taxation, your accountant can set up a form that shows the gross and net income delivered by the properties you claim and ascertain what is expected.

A few states force authorizing charges for property proprietors, similar to a business permit due yearly based on your property's size or the income your properties create. States may likewise force permitting charges for rental property. In any case, the most well-known tax comes as a sum based on the income — net (all-out), not net (after costs) — that you've produced.

Federal Tax

Federal taxes influence everybody. You must record your government tax return on a yearly premise and account for your venture property income and costs. You may need to make good on income government obligation on net income, and that some might be not quite the same as what your companion is paying, based on the structure of your business and how you have claimed your property. There are numerous approaches to structure the set-up of your properties. You can have an association, a corporation, an LLC, a trust, and so forth. A decent accountant will encourage you based on your circumstance. For example, if your rental property is worked as a corporation, your accountant may prompt you not so toward the finish of every year; you ought not to have any income in your account to abstain from paying a high pace of corporate tax. (You don't need your corporation to be twofold taxed.) You can pull back the cash as income, spend it on enhancements to your structure, or take care of tabs. Your accountant realizes what is best for your business.

Property Tax

Property tax is typically an ad valorem (forced at a %age of the worth) that a proprietor of land or other property pays to estimate the property. A couple of state tax is based on the measure and utilization of the land. The taxing authority performs or requires an evaluation of the property's estimation, and the tax is surveyed to that worth. A significant fragment of nearby and legislative organizations get a considerable segment of their working assets by taxing land inside their purview. As a rule, the property tax increments as often as possible through a few extraordinary evaluation charges based on enhancements, voted-in measures, schools, or crisis administrations. These charges could be a %age or a level rate contingent upon how it was voted in by the individuals or legislative organization.

An expert appraiser, as a rule, surveys the property at the time you buy the property. It is to decide the worth based on the property and other similar properties in the region. There are three fundamental strategies for determining the honest estimation: the business correlation, the cost methodology, and the pay approach. The two appraisers and tax assessors, for the most part, utilize more than one of the above ways to deal with be sure the last gauge of significant worth is right. Remember that building and land are assessed independently. Most states have frameworks set up in which a property is reassessed or revalued intermittently. At that point, the higher your property is esteemed, the higher the property tax. Property taxes in many states are ordinarily paid two times every year.

Property tax is a huge, fixed cost. Even though taxes aren't charged month to month, you should represent them when you are doing your month to month planning. A few proprietors have the protection and taxes embedded in their home loan every month. It is an appropriate/escrow account and is one approach to guarantee you have the cash for these enormous entireties of cash due two times a year. Endeavor not to be late with your property tax payments, as the punishments are, as a rule, around 10 %. A few states enable you to charge the portions on a Visa at no extra charge. If you have an uncommon Visa where you amass focuses or carrier mileage every month based on your charges, your focus can include rapidly on your property taxes. Numerous banks address non-payment of property tax inside the advance administrative work and evaluate your advance, making it due and payable quickly on the off chance that you don't pay your taxes. A few regions likewise have individual property taxes. So on the off chance that you leave an icebox, washer/dryer, or other furnishings and installations in the property, you should report these too. As a rule, the best source is to contact the city or province government for a full rundown of taxes surveyed or ask your bookkeeper.

Transfer Tax

This tax is typically exacted at the time of a property deal. It is generally charged by the city and the rate shifts in every territory. This sum is usually taken out and represented in the escrow procedure of acquiring or selling any property

Depreciation

In figuring your tax commitment every year, the administration enables investment property proprietors to make a finding for depreciation. Comprehend that depreciation isn't an out-of-pocket cost you bring about. Or maybe, it is a bookkeeping idea that enables you to deduct typical mileage and is an approach to protect salary. It is intended to help with ordinary mileage as well as give you more income.

Paces of depreciation shift with the class and life expectancy of the asset.

For instance, a structure is depreciated over a long period, while a PC is depreciated over just a couple of years. There are limits set by law concerning what extent the life expectancy for specific things is.

Try not to choose or figure without anyone else's input to what extent the asset should last. Converse with your bookkeeper.

Repairs Versus Renovations

The general principle is that fixed costs are tax-deductible in the year spent, while redesign costs are spread over the years.

Bigger things must be depreciated over the years, while the little things can be deducted entirely promptly from that year's tax return.

Passive Versus Active

It is essential to know the distinction from the IRS stance and for your tax purposes.

If you are in the matter of land and it is your essential vocation, there are no genuine limitations on the dollar measure of misfortunes you can guarantee and apply against your income.

A great many people consider their investment property as a discretionary calling. Provided that this is true, the IRS has a cutoff of $25,000 on yearly misfortune derivations. Generally speaking, if you are what some insinuate as a peaceful associate, you are an idle financial specialist.

As a detached financial specialist, you can use the decay thinking to adjust your property's profit.

By IRS rules, you are adequately connected with your speculation property's important initiative, paying little mind to whether you have a specialist organization association set up.

If you assist with choosing decisions considering critical fixes, last assurance of your occupants, or rental aggregates, you are seen as a functioning financial specialist.

There are numerous inventive approaches to guarantee you are getting every one of the focal points and full benefits accessible through your learned bookkeeper.

Investment strategies: How to grow your portfolio

As a focused real estate investor, you should start planning to build a real estate portfolio if you want to accumulate long-term wealth even though you're just starting. What is a real estate portfolio? A real estate portfolio is the summation of all your investment property, which you have acquired and are still managing, intending to get high financial returns. A real estate portfolio shows how much you've diversified in purchasing real estate assets. A well-diversified portfolio would include rental properties and real estate investment trusts, and even flipping houses. Before making a move to grow your real estate portfolio, you need to set your goals. How long will it take you to achieve them? What risks are you willing to take to ensure you reap full rewards? Can you risk losing some of your original investment to get more profits?

What does an investment portfolio include?

Besides the "resume" of investment assets you have acquired, your portfolio should also include testimonials from your former lenders. It would help you secure more funding for future investment deals. The collection should also include your buying philosophy. Someone looking at your portfolio should see your investment goals and strategies where you've succeeded and failed. When building a real estate investment portfolio, consider the following concepts:

Objective

Do you have an investment goal? What is the drive behind the type of property you purchased? You need to understand your end goal to know the kind of assets you want to add to your portfolio.

Do you want to go for short term gains such as wholesaling, flipping, or Airbnb? Or do you want investments that will guarantee you long term gains like rental properties?

Although it's good to diversify, you should be careful when making an investment choice, because your options will help you achieve your financial goal. You don't want an investment that will harm your bottom line.

Figures

Your real estate investment portfolios should include all your investment assets with accurate figures such as the purchase price, transaction cost, holding cost, repair cost, sales price, and profit.

All the data should appear in your portfolio to show whoever cares to see that you're transparent. Whether the profit or sales price looks good or embarrassing, you should add them.

Also, include your financing details. How did you get the financing for your investment assets? How was it structured? How did you find a seller for your property? The details you include here will depend on your investment strategy.

Other figures, the portfolio should have been monthly operating costs and improvement costs. These are the repairs and renovations you did on the property before and after purchase. Provide a summary of the expenses, including the after-repair value. The figures should clearly state how costs turn into profits for you.

Asset Allocation

Here you'll need to add assets that will help you accomplish your financial goals. The assets you choose should depend on your investment strategy and your risk tolerance.

Do you prefer to play it safe by buying properties from your state, or can you go out of state? Would you rather invest in residential or commercial rental properties? Remember, if you seek more significant returns, you should be willing to take more risks. Nothing comes easy.

Management

Your portfolio should give insights on how you take care of your investment properties. Did you hire a property manager, or did you self-manage all? If you self-manage, including how you were able to handle the property all by yourself.

If you had hired a property manager, how much did it cost? If you're going to apply for a loan to expand your portfolio, your prospective lender would like to see how you managed your properties in the past.

Why you should build a real estate investment portfolio

Buying one or two investment properties is great, but you will reap lots of financial benefits when you focus on building a real estate portfolio. With the steady cash flow you get from the investments, and you can pay the mortgage you used to purchase your rental property.

With time, your property can appreciate, making it more profitable and able to withstand inflation. Most importantly, having a portfolio gives you multiple tax benefits compared to when you have just one investment.

What are the tax benefits of building a rental property portfolio?

The expenses you spend after purchasing your rental property are tax-deductible. You can discount some figures from your transactions so long you keep your receipts safe. Some of the expenses that are deductible includes

- Mortgage interest

- Advertising

- Commissions paid to rental agents

- Cleaning and maintenance

- Utilities

- Insurance premiums

- Homeowner association (HOA fees)/condo dues

- Legal fees

- Taxes

Real estate investments to grow your portfolio

Aside from the residential rental properties, which most beginning investors focus their investment strength on, there are other alternatives you can use to expand your portfolio. Remember, diversification is key.

Commercial Real Estate

Commercial properties are naturally the following step for any investor interested in investing in rental properties. They bring higher profits when compared to residential properties. You can add it to your portfolio if you're looking to diversify.

Reits

Real Estate Investment Trusts are the easiest way to build your portfolio without purchasing the properties yourself.

You only need to invest in the companies responsible for purchasing the properties, and then you earn your dividend. So now, you're not only earning income from your properties, but you're also earning from a well-structured organization. A win-win situation.

Raw Land

You can buy and hold a raw land until it appreciates before selling it again. Or you can develop it and lease it out to renters. You can even divide it and resell it. Most experienced rental property investors are now adding this to their portfolio. You should consider it too when you're ready.

Lessons To Take Away

Building your portfolio requires a lot of work, especially when you are purchasing assets you plan on keeping a long time (buy and hold). Your properties should have a low vacancy rate, and the management and maintenance should be on point.

Remember to keep cash reserves as this would come in handy to fix unexpected damages and general maintenance, especially when your property isn't occupied.

You also have the task of screening people who wish to rent your property thoroughly. Your tenants can either make or mar your property investments, so you need to take great care.

Also, ensure you're earning valuable rental income from them. Check how much you spend on monthly expenses, then subtract from your rental income to see if you're getting value from your rental properties.

A real estate portfolio is not something that you can build overnight. It requires time and focuses. You need to be strategic about the investments you're adding to your portfolio too.

When you take your time to grow your portfolio, you'll see how easy it becomes getting funding or closing new deals. You can use your portfolio as leverage to get better deals.

Diversifying your portfolio can also help to mitigate risks. Even as a beginner investor, reading and hearing all the stories from experienced investors, you should have realized that investing in real estate is not all sunshine. It comes with a lot of risks. And the higher your quest for returns, the higher the risk.

However, when you have different real estate assets under your belt, you can mitigate risks, since all your eggs are not in a single basket.

For example, if you've invested in residential and commercial real estate, if the market crashes affect residential properties, you can still earn rental income from commercial properties.

Finally, while building your portfolio, try as much as possible to avoid mistakes, other experienced investors have spoken about.

Connect with them through networking and learn from them. Avoid common mistakes like not doing your due diligence before purchasing a property, not working with real estate professionals, underestimating expenses, and of course, refusing to diversify your portfolio.

Four things successful real estate investors have in common

What are the key traits of successful real estate investors? Why do they keep making lots of money off real estate while some other investors count their losses and regret ever investing in real estate? What are they doing differently?

How are they beating the overwhelming competition the real estate market is facing with lots of people joining? What do you need to do as a beginner investor to join the league of successful real estate investors in no time?

They Are Knowledgeable

You can't be successful at something when you don't have in- depth knowledge about it. In the real estate investment world, knowing your market is essential. You can make informed business decisions when you are aware of the current trends in the market.

If you aspire to be a successful investor, you should have at your fingertips current demands, consumer habits, mortgage rates, and other significant factors that affect the real estate market.

When you keep tabs on changes going on in the market, you'll be able to predict future changes, which will help your investment strategy and prevent costly mistakes.

Learn about the language of real estate. Know the meaning of terms like cap rate, rental income, expenses, cash on cash returns, property tax, tax deductions, etc. Know the legal implications of acquiring properties. Find out the laws of different states that are suitable for investment. Don't be caught on the wrong side of the law. Ignorance is never an excuse.

Build Their Network

We have always stressed the importance of having a real estate network as an investor. Every business person knows the need to build a strong network, and if you're yet to treat your investments as a business, you're not serious about it.

As a real estate investor, you need to include networking into your investment strategy to ensure that you get to know people relevant to your business and get to know you.

You can get your hands-on resources that could expand your investment portfolio by networking with the right people.

You gain referrals, advice, consultation, and everything you need to succeed: the bigger your network, the more opportunities you have to increase your business.

Ensure you're noticed, and other investors feel your presence.

Break the ice and introduce yourself, build, and maintain that relationship. Connect with every real estate professional that can help you expand your business portfolio.

See It As A Business

Whether you agree or not, investing in real estate is a business of its own since you're going to record profit and loss in every transaction. And if you're going to be successful in this field, you need to see it that way. Treat your investments the same way you'll treat a business venture.

Make plans, whether it's short term or long term. Know your goals and objectives, and strategize how you can meet them. After accomplishing a goal, start planning for another one.

Ensure your business is well-organized and structured. You might not need the bureaucracy and hierarchy, but you sure need professionals to make your investments run smoothly.

Hire the necessary professionals such as a real estate agent, broker, property manager, lawyer, accountant, etc.

Monitor your finances, always have your cash reserves for unexpected expenses and downtimes.

Focus on scaling your business and watch how you expand your investment portfolio with ease.

Keep Track Of Numbers

Using your guts is good, but only when you do not have numbers to work with. As long as there are tools for researching, analyzing, and comparing, keep your guts aside and focus on the numbers.

Always do your estimates. When considering the property's value, don't hesitate to walk if the numbers do not add up.

Negotiation and Risks of Rental Property Investing

Master the art of Successful Negotiation

Negotiation will become your best friend. It's something you should learn inside and out because everything is negotiable, especially in real estate.

There are several things you can discuss on - the final price of the property you're interested in, what conditions you want for the payment, how long of a payment period you'd like, how much you're renting it out for, even the furniture and various objects that can come with the property. You want the best deal possible, once that leaves you feeling satisfied and proud of yourself when investing in a property.

However, negotiation is a skill, one that you'll get better with as time goes on. You'll learn the various tips and tricks, and what works for you and what doesn't. It can be problematic when you're just starting, but as you get more experience in real estate investing, you'll also get more experienced in negotiating.

Tips to Be a Better Negotiator Finances

You don't want to spend more than you can afford, and sometimes that happens when you're negotiating. Work it out your finances before going into the negotiation. Identify how much cash you have available and any other means of money. Make a budget, and see how much potential spending you'd do for the property, how much money you have available at this exact moment, and how much of a profit you'd expect to make.

You need to be profitable from the very first month, or else your business can easily fail. Once you've put together your budget, you know the exact number you can't go over when negotiating. Focus on the properties you can afford, and go back to the more expensive ones after you can realistically afford them.

Analyze

After figuring out the property you want to invest in, and once you're ready to move forward, the best step you can take is analyzing the real estate market in the area. You need to work out what the surrounding properties are going for or how much they've sold for in the past few weeks/months. Look at the selling prices, not the asking prices.

The selling prices are a better example of what your new property is worth and how much you can realistically expect to ask for when negotiating. Keep that number in mind when going throughout the negotiating process and be firm!

Identify

You need to work it out if you're working in a buyer's or seller's market. One is better for you, but you can still be successful in negotiations if you know ahead of time which market is trending at the moment. To know for sure, look at how many properties are listed in your area, how long they've been on the market, how much they're going for, the difference in listing and selling price, and the closing percentage. There's a big difference when investing in a property if it's a buyer's market. You're able to take a lot more time before you close on the deal, you have the opportunity to counter with a lower price than is originally asked, and you can even ask for some things that would be a lot more beneficial to you. On the opposite side, however, things are a lot different when it's a seller's market. You have to act swiftly, be ready to pay a higher price than originally asked, offer more beneficial conditions to the former owner and remember not to expect a lot to come with the property. What makes things a lot more difficult is that competition is much fiercer with other buyers, so you have to act quickly and won't bargain when doing negotiations.

Real Estate Agent

Although you might not want to spend the upfront costs of hiring a real estate agent, it's worth it if you want the best deal possible. It is even more pertinent if you're a newbie and don't know what you're doing. A real estate agent can make the negotiation process run smoothly and takes over the negotiations completely. Some people tend to be more introverted, so if you don't want to deal with negotiations or speak to the seller directly, then a real estate agent makes sense! Plus, an agent is much less likely to make a mistake if you're just starting. You can learn from them and once you know more, then try the negotiations yourself.

The Why

Why is the seller selling? It's best to know the reasons before negotiating because it will give you leverage going in. Maybe they just want to be closer to family, or maybe there's something seriously wrong with the property. If it's the latter, then you can renegotiate the selling price to go way down, which would be in your favor. And knowing why they're selling helps you know when to press harder in your negotiations and back down.

Negotiate, Negotiate, Negotiate!

When investing in real estate business, the key to getting the best possible deal and benefiting your business is to remember that you can negotiate everything, not just the price. You can try to negotiate the closing costs and date, the warranties, repairs, if the owner can leave any appliances or furniture, etc.

Basically everything! It's especially helpful if the market is trending at a seller's market, and you might not get the exact price you wanted. Instead, you can try for a deal that everyone's happy with by getting different types of benefits. Investing in rental property is all about the long term, so those extra benefits might end up putting a higher value on your property. If you choose to auction the house, you could end up getting a great little profit.

Compromise

It can be hard to compromise, especially if you've had your heart set on a certain price and if you tend to lean towards the stubborn side. You want to negotiate in a way where everyone ends up happy, not just you. Look at the surrounding homes that have sold recently, and negotiate the price to reflect that. For example, let's say a home nearby sold for $600,000, and it doesn't have any add-ons, like a pool, fireplace, etc. But the property you're looking at investing in has all that, plus more. So, it's not a smart business decision to try and buy that property for less than $600,000; there's no way the seller will want to sell it at that price or even negotiate. They'll just move on to the following buyer and pass you up. And if you've found a property that you like, then don't pay more than you're willing actually to pay.

While it's important to make sure the seller is happy, you need to compromise yourself. If you just can't reach a good price for both you and the seller, then remember it's ok to walk away. It isn't going to be your home, and it's your business. And you need to make decisions that are good for your business and make sense specifically from an investor's viewpoint.

Potential Risks of Rental Property Investing

There are advantages to investing in rental properties. You can earn a lot of passive income and make great profits, all while maintaining financial security for the future. And while owning rental properties can be relatively safe, there are risks involved. It's good to practice diligence and ensure that you'll know how to turn it around quickly before losing any money if any of the negatives happen.

Vacancy

Having a high amount of vacancies is probably one of the worst things to happen to a rental property owner. Tenants are how you make your money and income, so going without them means you go without money. You can even reach a negative cash flow, meaning you have to start paying out of pocket for expenses. It can add up, and you end up losing a ton of money that you won't be able to make back. The best way to avoid this from happening or lessen the blow is by purchasing rental properties in good neighborhoods. Do the proper research about the different areas; work out which neighborhoods are safest, and yield the best amenities. Keeping a saving specifically for vacancies would probably be the smart thing to do, just if you end up having to pay the mortgage, insurance, and property taxes from your own money.

Bad Tenants

While dealing with vacancies can mean you might lose money, having bad tenants can be so much worse. There's a large risk when taking in unknown people, and it requires you to be pretty selective. You need to do a thorough background checks, get references from former landlords, ask for proof of income, run a credit check, and make sure to take a security deposit.

Cash Flow

Triple check the expenses and how much everything will cost you; even put in the cost of random maintenance that might never happen. Underestimating the cost could mean the end of your business, and you owe thousands of dollars. It's not just considering the upfront costs, but how much everything will cost you each month.

If you end up losing money every month because of not realizing the cost, you'll eventually be out of business from paying out of pocket.

The Right Time to Buy

Just like in other markets, the real estate market also has a sort of supply and demand. There's a constant fluctuate, so if you're thinking of maybe selling your property down the road, you might end up not making a profit. Investing in rental properties can cost a lot of money, especially upfront, so you want to make sure that your expected return in the future makes it worth investing in the first place. The best method to do is see if it's a seller's or buyer's market, and keep up with the trends.

Theft

There's always a risk of your property becoming burglarized, especially if you're in a lower income location. If the crime rate is on the higher side, you'll end up with a high turnover of tenants.

Plus, you charge for rent will be much lower than what you could charge in a higher income location. If burglary does happen a lot in your location, you could end up paying a lot of money in legal procedures and fees.

Foreclosure

If you end up not making enough profit, and can't meet your mortgage payments, then there's the change of your property being foreclosed. It's the last thing you want because not only can it hurt you being approved for any future real estate loans, but the word might get around, and no one would want to rent from you.

Maintenance

There's a high level of work involved when running rental properties, and that included maintenance issues. Knowing basic maintenance can be very helpful as a landlord, and help you save spending more money on issues that end up becoming a lot worse. Or if you're not very handy, you can hire a property manager who knows how to fix those types of things. Keep in mind too that, eventually, properties start to show their age. They typically start having structural damage, and major things would need replacing.

Airbnb

There's some risk of renting out property specifically for short-term rent, like Airbnb. You can make a lot of money doing it, but sometimes the local authorities put forth certain laws and restrictions for these businesses. You have to make sure that you pay all the different fees and taxes, and learn all the different local state and city laws about short-term rentals.

To Flip Or Not To Flip

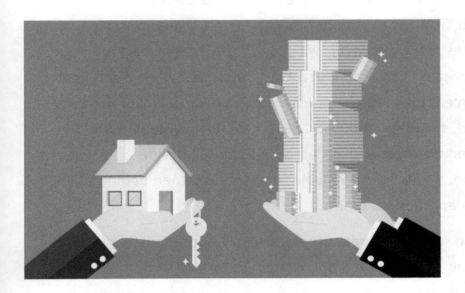

Flipping a house is the process of buying a house and fixing it up and intending to sell it for a profit. It can also be used successfully by people who want to get into

the real estate rents property game. House flipping is about as basic as you can get in the world of real estate investing. To be a successful flipper, you will want to buy at a low price, fix it up reasonably, and sell it at a high price.

You will need to carefully research the local market before you decide to buy a project house. Every market will not be suitable for your house flipping journey. It is why you should decide on your budget before you buy it. If you only have a budget of twenty thousand dollars, you will not be looking at houses that cost seven hundred thousand dollars. When you have less on-hand cash to work with, you will need to be more careful. Financing for an investment property will cover the major part of your purchase. Still, there is a big difference between a twenty percent down payment for a fifty-thousand- dollar property and a twenty thousand dollar down payment for a five hundred-thousand-dollar property. So, decide how much money you have available to spend and then begin to pick the appropriate market.

One way many real estate investors go about finding the right neighborhood is to classify the possible neighborhoods as A, B, C, and D. Neighborhoods that are in Class A are the wealthiest neighborhoods the housing market offers you. These are the neighborhoods that are inhabited by high- income professional people. Class B neighborhoods are those that are populated by solid middle-class families. Blue-collar neighborhoods are the Class C neighborhoods, filled with working-class people. The bottom of the neighborhood class ladder is the Class D neighborhood, which houses the lower- income earners. The crucial key to success will be to choose the neighborhood where your money can do the best and where you feel the most comfortable. You might have the financial resources to flip houses in the Class A neighborhood, but do you feel comfortable there? Are you happy looking at high-end finishes and planning myriads of one-use rooms for a potential buyer? Or are you more comfortable in the Class C or D neighborhood where you might be doing a real service for good people looking for a house to rent? Either way is just fine, but you need to decide which way is best for you before buying your first property.

Class D neighborhoods might come with their own set of anomalies. They may come with risks not found in the other neighborhood types. Insurance premiums might be higher for these houses because the crime rate might be higher or give the impression of being higher. Remember that it is not always the act that drives the cost of insurance but the act's possibility. A house being flipped in a Class D neighborhood might be more likely to be vandalized or burglarized.

A property located in a Class B or C neighborhood might be the best location for your first flip. These are solidly middle class and stable working-class neighborhoods that will usually have a lower rate of crime involved. A flipped house that is structurally sound and cosmetically attractive will entice renters to move there relatively easily. When you choose your first house to flip, try to look for houses that only require cosmetic updates. Replacing a few fixtures in the bathroom and kitchen, new cabinets, fresh paint and flooring, and a little curb appeal, these will get you the biggest return on your investment and will get you a house suitable for renting in the shortest amount of time. Eventually, you will purchase a more complicated flip or that you are not qualified to do it. But the first house needs to be relatively easy for several reasons. An easier house to flip will cost less money, and it will build your confidence. And a house that is ready quickly is one you won't get tired of and can be used as leverage in your next real estate deal.

When you have successfully flipped your first few houses, then you can look at more complicated flips. But you do not want to deal with structural issues like a cracked or sinking foundation in the beginning. You also don't want to deal with mechanical issues like replacing the HVAC (heating, ventilation, air conditioning) system or relocating the electrical system's breaker box. Both of these involve pulling permits, getting permission from the local government to do the work. Then someone from the proper governmental agency will come out to inspect the work. It type of flip will come in time; be patient.

Ensure that your fund is in place before looking at properties so that when you find a good one, you will be ready to make an offer. Because if you find a flip that will be a good deal, then someone else will find it a good deal, too. When you purchase a house that needs rehab work, you don't get a mortgage loan, and you get a bridge loan. Its loan will "bridge" the time between buying the property and selling the property. If you decide to keep the property, which is the main goal of this exercise, you will replace the bridge loan with a mortgage loan.

It is the time when you will need to hire a contractor or build relationships with several contractors. If it is at all possible, go to sites they are working on so that you can see some of their work. It is a good idea to get several bids for rehabbing the property even before you make an offer on the property. If the bids you are getting are way out of line than what you were planning to spend, maybe this is not the house for you. And whatever budget amount you settle on, add twenty percent to that amount. It will cover any unexpected costs that might come up. For example, when pulling out the kitchen cabinets to replace them, you might damage the wall behind the sink that will need to be fixed. It might be easier to replace the wallboard than to spend the time removing the wallpaper that seems to have been there forever. It extra twenty percent is your contingency fund, in case things happen you weren't expecting.

Flipping houses is a worthless venture if you do not know how to find the house in the first place. And you will want to find a good deal. Your realtor might be able to help you find a house that needs a little loving to be beautiful again.

And since you are just starting, it might be a good idea to remain close to home. Since you already live in the neighborhood, then you should already know plenty of information about it.

Finding a flip in your personal, geographic region gives you several advantages. As we said, you already know the neighborhood.

You will know better than most which parts of town are still popular for people to move into and which parts have lately become more unfavorable.

You will understand the attractions of the neighborhood and the local culture. It will mean that you will have a better knowledge of the home's value besides the numbers on paper.

Living close physically to your project will make it much more convenient for you to get to work and to be able to oversee the project.

It alone will save you money and time. If the project is close by, you will regularly see the project if you do not actively work on it during the rehab project. It will allow you to meet with the contractors and sub-contractors regularly. And you will be nearby to show the home to potential renters, something that your property manager will do for you when you hire them, in addition to overseeing the renovation. By taking care of the first few projects yourself, you will understand the kind of performance you will expect from your manager.

When you plan your renovations and look at material prices, make sure you prepare a good estimate of the overall cost to set a proper budget.

When you pick out what looks like the perfect floor time, don't forget to price the glue, grout, baseboard, and tools you might need. And if someone else is laying this floor tile, you will need to pay for that person's labor bill.

When we say stick to easy rehabilitation, the easiest projects will bring you the biggest financial return. You might need to replace all the cabinets, appliances, and fixtures in the kitchen and bathrooms, but if you keep the existing floor plan and go with builder's grade fixtures, you can do all of this for very little money. Put fresh paint on the walls and lay new flooring.

Going with laminate over carpet is the better choice for rental housing because the floors are easier to maintain and won't stain or hold odors like carpet will. Don't overlook things like outlet covers and wall switch covers; replacing them is inexpensive but will make the walls look finished.

Anything that you are not painting or replacing will need to be scrubbed meticulously, especially the windows. Dirt will not look attractive to a potential renter.

No matter what kind and style of fixtures you choose for this house, the most important piece of advice ever is to maximize the potential of your return by limiting the amount of financial risk you take. It simply means not paying too much for the house you buy, and this requires knowing what the house will be worth when it is finished and the potential cost of the needed repairs.

When you have this information, you will then be better able to decide on an excellent purchase price.

Pay close attention to the seventy percent rule. That rule states that you should not pay more than seventy percent of the house's after-repair value.

It is the value of the house after the house is repaired fully. Think of it this way: if the home's after-repair value is one hundred thousand dollars and the house needs twenty-five thousand dollars' worth of repair work, then according to the seventy percent rule, you should not pay more than forty-five thousand dollars for the house.

$100,000 x 70% = $70,000 - $25,000 = $45,000

The after-repair value is the value that the house would sell for if you were going to sell it. So since you are flipping this house to keep and rent to a tenant, then you have just paid forty-five thousand dollars for a house that could potentially be worth one hundred thousand dollars, which is instant equity in your pocket.

Flipping houses is a business venture, just like owning real estate for rental property is. Just like being a landlord, flipping houses is the kind of business that will require effort, skill, patience, planning, money, and time.

It will most likely end up being more expensive and more difficult than what you ever expected it to be. And even the flippers and landlords who get every detail just right can sometimes fail. It is not a quick scheme for you to get rich but a steady lifelong plan to grow your wealth.

Neal Hooper

Common Mistakes That You Need to Avoid

Each retail investor dreams of beginning a real estate investment business, making money, and enjoying the "good life." Many fail to realize that investing in real

estate can be incredibly complicated and expensive if you don't know what you're doing. When you take it slowly and know how to do it properly, it can be very lucrative to invest in real estate.

Mistake #1:

Failure to Invest in Education. Attempt to invest in infrastructure before you start paying your rent, and you need to take time to learn the fundamentals of investing in real estate. It does not mean that you need to spend thousands on training or courses related to "guru;" it means that you have to spend time researching the various investment strategies to understand what you need to do to succeed.

Mistake #2:

Failure to set up a business. Several people begin investing with their cash, name, and credit on a small scale. What they cannot know is that any mistake could cost you all you've worked so hard to make.

Use your homework and produce a business entity that best suits your needs before you start investing. In most instances, the most appropriate company to use for your corporation will be an LLC or a Company. If something goes wrong down the road, you can cover your assets in creating a business company.

Mistake #3:

Depending on the type of assets you own, and what you plan to do with the property, the type of coverage you will need will be decided. If you're planning to buy a single-family home for sale, you'll need to get a rental agreement. If you plan to buy and sell "Flip" property, a General Commercial Cost Plan may be the way to go as many will cover the deal's cost. For best practice, make sure that you will need you to talk to a professional insurance agent when determining which type of insurance you will need.

Mistakes#4:

Failure to Strategize & Plan. Real Estate Investing is like any other company, so why don't you treat it like one? You need to build a clear plan of action to proceed if you want to be successful. Decide which strategy(s) works best for you before you start investing. Don't panic if it takes a while to determine the right plan, but make sure that you stick with it when you find it out.

Mistakes#5:

Failure to find and manage a budget. One of the first things you need to do is find out how much cash you need to spend. If you only have enough money for a condo, don't try to buy an apartment complex. Once you've worked out how much money you've got to spend, concentrate your time and energy on a budget that fits your needs. If you're over-budgeting, your growth potential may be reduced. If you're under budget, you're most likely going to get into trouble, resulting in a large amount of debt.

Mistake #6:

Failure to Correctly Estimate the Cost of Repairs. Not only will this mistake cost you time, but it can also cost you the whole deal. Invest in a local contractor to inspect the property to provide you with a list of improvements that will be required and the cost of completing every repair if you are looking to purchase a house. It will save you time on the back end and thousands of dollars.

Mistake #7:

Failure to create a team. Everyone heard the saying, "You're just as good as the weakest link." If you're trying to invest in real estate and don't have a strong team behind you, you will be the weakest link. It is essential to surround yourself with a great group of people and to continue to have an excellent working relationship with these people. Developing your team can take a lot of time and energy, but demonstrate your progress when you're finished.

Mistake #8:

Failure to take action. After educating yourself, starting a business, securing insurance, defining a strategy or project, developing a budget, and establishing your team, nothing is left to put everything to work and take action. At first, it might be daunting. You might make little mistakes, but if you don't take action, you're never going to make money and be successful. It can be challenging to invest in real estate, and if you go wrong, it can be costly. Investing in real estate, on the other hand, can be very professional and financially beneficial. Don't be afraid to ask a specialist for assistance. If you know what you're doing, most of these errors can be prevented. The more information you acquire and research, the fewer errors you make.

How to Automate Your Rental Investing Business

One thing you'll see when you invest in Real Estate is that there's a lot of work to do to get a deal done, and the weather you're a rehabber or a wholesaler, and you've got to do a lot of work before it's sold. You usually have more time than cash at the start of most shareholder companies, and you end up doing everything yourself to keep down your costs and increase your profits. Heck, marketing itself is costly enough, and if you have little or no money to start with, you're forced to do all you can to get your first contract.

That's fine, and nearly everyone starts that way, but you don't always want to stay that way, even if by doing so, you can make a more significant piece of the pie. But why is this? If I could save money and make more per deal, why wouldn't I want to do it all myself? There's a straightforward reason why you want to pay someone else to do certain things and why working on others is essential to you. The simple answer is not the same as all the tasks of an investment real estate business. Saying the same word in another way, some jobs are simple enough that anyone can do them while others need the ability to think, invent, lead, and communicate.

And back to my original question as to why you don't want to do this independently. Focusing on essential tasks and contracting out the bottom and eventually, middle-level tasks for others is simply more productive. It is attributable to something called "hourly pay." When you spread your time doing all aspects of the business, you take your hourly wage and average it from the whole pie. If, on the other hand, you only perform the essential tasks and contract the rest at a low price, you will produce more, and your hourly wage will rise. It is the main difference between a sole owner and a businessman and why the businessman ends up making money. I don't know about you, but I got to make money and have a ton of free time in this business!

Let me give you an excellent example of what I'm thinking about. My husband and I primarily sell the MLS and Craigslist in two different locations to find all of our offers. Both of these places are necessarily free to market (yes, I know the MLS costs money every year, but let's say it's free from there... deal? after the fee is paid). And, every day, we can spend hours sending lowball deals to the MLS and advertising on Craigslist to get people to call in. Then every day, we can spend hours dealing with Realtors ' answers and sellers ' calls. All you need to find a deal, and that's when it all happens at once! Now you're having to do daily tasks like putting up advertisements and making offers on the MLS, coping with emails and calls in addition to putting together the deal so that you can either sell or rehabilitate it. What's most likely to happen is that the lower tier activities cease while you're focused on the tasks that make you money, and when you make that money, you've got to start all over again.

Here is what I suggest, hire a Virtual Assistant after you make your first or even second deal, and you've got some money to play with now! When we did that, our production skyrocketed, and there was a decrease in the amount of work we had to do, and all that work was the tedious work we hated doing! Now we have a lady over in India who works for $2.25 an hour with a Masters's degree making offers on the MLS. Have you heard me there? She's got a Master Dang, and she's working for

$2.25 an hour!

Try to see if you can get a homeless man to work for the cheap one. Ha! Even if you could bet a month's wages, he wouldn't put in the same effort and enthusiasm as the lady with her degree we have in India;) She's extraordinarily productive and very smart and can send 50-60 offers to the MLS within 2 hours. We started working 10 hours a week with her, and she was worth her gold weight! Think about it, and we've got about 250-300 deals for about $25 each week. We made her do more research as time went by, while we focused on the creative tasks (which are also more enjoyable and take less time) high!

Necessarily, Virtual Assistants are people who can perform any function you request of them that can be done on an internet-connected device. Someone who sends an offer to the MLS or places an ad on Craigslist does NOT have to be in my office, nor do I have to see them know they are doing their job. We let her use our company email to send deals, and we can track her progress by merely checking the sent folder to see what she's doing so limited oversight. So, anywhere in the world, this person can be! How many of us wanted to work with our jobs from home, but it never seemed that the bosses were on board for it?

We can now be the "hot" boss and, as a result, reap the rewards! You can do all the menial tasks once you have someone on board and let you concentrate on the things that will make you money, like bringing together buyers and sellers! The larger you get, the more tasks you need your Virtual Assistant to delegate. You can eventually get an "apprentice" real estate investor who can do everything you need, including managing your Virtual Assistant. A wage plus a percentage of profits can be paid to him.

Pay Fewer Taxes and Keep More of Your Money

Like all other kinds of income, taxes eat into investment profits. While you probably can't avoid them completely, there are a lot of things you can do to keep

the tax bite as small as possible. In fact, in some cases, real estate investments may produce tax losses even when you're collecting cash—it's one of their greatest potential benefits. Take time to learn the ins and outs of real estate tax rules, or find a tax preparer experienced in this area. There are lots of loopholes to take advantage of...if you know exactly where to look.

Special Real Estate Tax Rules

Building Tax Shelters

On top of all the income and cash flow real estate investments can generate; they also come with special tax benefits that can save you a lot of money. The Tax Cuts and Jobs Act of 2017 were kind to real estate investors and especially advantageous to landlords. The new law protects some old advantages unique to real estate investment and adds a wealth of new benefits. That said, the new tax law isn't yet fully understood; it's important to enlist professional tax help to make sure you take advantage of every possible deduction. It could take years for the IRS to figure out how they'll interpret some of the new rules, so ensure your tax preparer knows the most current rulings.

Special Deductions And Benefits

Real estate investing comes with several tax benefits that simply aren't available for other types of investments. Depreciation—an on-paper expense that reduces taxable income and ends up providing positive cash flow—is the one most people know about, but there are more. For example, a unique "trading up" provision called 1031 exchanges lets you sell and buy property without paying capital gains taxes on profits. Another bonus: passive earnings (like real estate investing) aren't subject to Social Security and Medicare taxes, another huge savings.

Special Rules For REIT Dividends

REIT investors will get extra benefits from the new tax laws (the Tax Cuts and Jobs Act, or TCJA), making REITs an even better investment option. Unlike "qualified" stock dividends that get taxed at special more-favorable rates, the dividends from REITs get sliced and diced into three categories that determine their tax treatment. The categories work like this:

- Ordinary income, which is taxed at your regular income tax rate

- Capital gains distributions, which get taxed at favorable long-term capital gains tax rates that top out at 20 percent

- Return of capital, which isn't taxable now, but could increase your capital gains tax bill when you sell the investment

It sounds complicated, but it will all be laid out on the single Form 1099-DIV you receive from the REIT. And if you're holding REITs in your retirement account (especially a highly tax-beneficial Roth IRA), you won't have to worry about it at all.

Long-Term Capital Gains

Other than house flipping, real estate investments are normally held long term. When they're eventually sold, they qualify for long-term capital gains rates, which are much lower than ordinary income tax rates.

What's A Capital Gain?

Capital assets are owned for longer than one year and not sold in the normal business (like inventory in a shop). When you sell a capital asset for more than you paid for it (i.e., you make a profit), you have a capital gain.

Any property you hold for longer than one year before selling it gets the long-term capital gains treatment. Depending on your filing status and income, your rate will be either 0 percent, 15 percent, or 20 percent. For example, if you file as single, and your taxable income is below $38,600, you would pay no taxes, 0 percent, on any long-term capital gains.

Bonus Depreciation For Landlords

There's a special tax provision called Sector 179 that lets business owners deduct 100 percent of personal property (such as desks and computers) in the year it was bought instead of depreciating it over time. In the past, rental property owners weren't allowed to use this provision for personal property (such as appliances, carpets, and furniture) in their rental units. The Tax Cuts and Jobs Act (TCJA) removed that restriction, and now landlords can take full advantage of Sector 179 deductions, up to a total of $1 million (but the deduction can't create a net loss).

The TCJA also offers an added "bonus depreciation." Before TCJA, business owners were limited to a bonus depreciation of up to 50 percent of a new asset's cost in the year it was purchased. Now bonus depreciation has been expanded to 100 percent and can be used for existing assets as well.

I know it sounds like Sector 179 and bonus depreciation is the same. Still, they have two very important differences: there's no annual limit on bonus depreciation (unlike the $1 million limits under Sector 179), and bonus depreciation is not limited to the profits (meaning it can create a net loss). These deductions can be tricky to maneuver, so talk to a pro.

While these bonuses help landlords, they also can help increase cash flows for indirect real estate investors. By increasing paper expenses to lower tax burdens, more money is available to pass through to investors.

The New 20 Percent Rule

The TCJA created a tax treasure for pass-through business owners, such as landlords set up as sole proprietorships, LLCs, and partnerships. Any profits earned through the rental properties get "passed through" to your income tax return. If your rental properties qualify as a business for tax purposes— and they almost always do when you actively participate in the business—the new tax law lets you deduct 20 percent of your net rental income from your taxable income. It can translate into huge tax savings, freeing up more money so you can beef up your investments or pay down some debt.

Be aware that this new twist is untested, and the 20 percent deduction is reserved for businesses. If you own rental properties but aren't at all involved in the business of dealing with them, that wouldn't qualify for this deduction. But if you do participate in a meaningful way (which could mean anything from taking care of maintenance to screening tenants on your own), you probably will be able to take advantage of it. Talk with a qualified CPA before you decide to take the 20 percent; if you take it when you're not supposed to, the IRS will tack on a 10 percent penalty.

Pass-Through Math

Let's say you have one rental property, a single-family home. During the year, your tenants paid $30,000 in rent. Your expenses as a landlord (including mortgage interest, property taxes, and depreciation) came to $20,000. It means you earned $10,000 in profits ($30,000 – $20,000) from that property. Its profit gets added to your other income, and you pay tax on your total income at the applicable tax rates.

But under TCJA, you can deduct 20 percent of that profit, or

$2,000, from your total income (if your rental property qualifies as a business). Instead of paying tax on the full

$10,000 of rental profits, you only have to pay tax on $8,000. Depending on your tax rate, that could save you hundreds, even thousands, of dollars on your tax bill.

The Rules

To qualify for that generous 20 percent deduction, you have to pass a few tests. First is the active participation test (you have to "work" at your rental properties). An income test: your taxable income has to be less than $157,500 if you're single and less than $315,000 if you're married (filing jointly) to take the full deduction. It phases out entirely if your taxable income hits $207,500 for singles or $415,000 for couples. In some cases, the deduction may still be available for landlords if they meet certain other qualifications; check with your accountant if that's your situation.

Get To Know These Tax Forms Doing The Paperwork

If you're new to real estate investing (or investing in general), you'll need to familiarize yourself with some new tax forms, whether you DIY taxes or hire a professional (which probably makes sense for the first year). The three main IRS forms you may be working with include Schedules E, B, and D, and all three are easily available on the IRS website (www.irs.gov). Here's a quick breakdown of each form's purpose:

- Schedule E reports passive income from rental properties, partnerships, and trusts.

- Schedule B reports interest and dividend income.

- Schedule D reports capital gains and losses when you sell assets (like stocks, funds, or flip properties).

The forms can look complicated at first glance, but they're pretty straightforward. If you're doing your taxes, you'll need a higher level of DIY software than you probably used before; most of the basic versions don't come with all of these forms. The software will guide you through some questions, but they don't always cover everything, so it's good to know what should be on these forums.

Schedule E: Supplemental Income And Loss

When you invest in real property as a landlord, the IRS counts that as a passive activity (even if you're an active landlord), with all the income and expenses reported on Schedule E. However, if you're involved with short-term rentals (like Airbnb, for example), the IRS classifies that as a small business. In these cases, the income and loss would get reported on a different form (Schedule C), and you would be eligible for the 20 percent deduction.

Easy Record Tracking

Landlords need to keep track of ongoing rental income and expenses along with anything that changes the cost basis of their property.

What Counts As Income?

When you're a landlord, you collect a lot of money, but not all of it counts as income for tax purposes. What counts is any kind of rent payment, no matter when you receive it (even an advance).

Rental income also includes any extra money you receive from tenants to cover expenses (for example, they pay a portion of a utility bill). Other items that count as income include:

• Early cancellation fees (for tenants who don't stay for their whole lease)

• Monthly pet fees

• The value of services (like lawn care) performed by tenants in exchange for reduced rent

Any kind of tenant deposit (a security or pet deposit, for example) doesn't count as income, because it's not your money; you have to give it back. The exception: if you keep a portion of the security deposit when the tenant vacates to cover property damage, that will count as income.

The Fourteen-Day Rule

If you rent your home for fourteen days or less during the year, that income does not have to be reported to the IRS. On the flip side, you don't get to deduct any expenses you wouldn't normally deduct as a homeowner.

A Wealth of Deductible Expenses

Unlike the house you live in, practically every expense attached to your rental property counts as a deductible business expense for tax purposes. Expenses to deduct include:

- Mortgage interest

- Property taxes

- Insurance

- Homeowners association dues

- Advertising (to fill a vacancy)

- Utilities

- Repairs and maintenance

- Pest control

- Landscaping

- Trash pickup

- Depreciation

What doesn't count as an expense? Any major repairs or renovations you perform count as capital expenditures that get added to the property's cost basis, effectively reducing your taxable income when you eventually sell.

About the Author

Neal Hooper is an entrepreneur, investor and the author of bundle "Investing in Real Estate".

A leading authority figure in the world of business, money, finance, and wealth management. He graduated with honors in computer engineering and economics and lives with his wife Kristen in Los Angeles, CA.

Real estate has made him more money than he could ever have imagined, and now, he wants to give back to society. He has decided to put his experiences on paper and started writing books so that everyone gets an opportunity to benefit from his success.

Through his training and coaching programs, he has worked directly with thousands of aspiring investors to jumpstart their rental property journey.

Previously, Neal worked in several corporate real estate and finance roles at large private companies, including at a private equity investment firm covering a wide range of commercial real estate acquisitions.

He will guide you on your journey to financial freedom and early retirement.

CPSIA information can be obtained
at www.ICGtesting.com
Printed in the USA
BVHW062037010321
601387BV00007B/554

9 781914 085574